Copyright © 2024 by Ayana T. Hardaway, Ph.D.
Website: ayanathardaway.com
ISBN: 979-8-9901206-1-7

All Rights Reserved. No part of this publication may be reproduced, distributed, or transmitted in any form or by any means, including photocopying, recording, or other electronic or mechanical methods, without the prior written permission of the publisher, except in the case of brief quotations embodied in critical reviews and certain other noncommercial uses permitted by copyright law. For more information on purchases in bulk or speaking events, please contact Ayana T. Hardaway at ayanathardaway.com.

Table of Contents

How to Use This Journal……………………………………5

Introduction…………………………………………………7

Chapter 1 Remember to Talk Back…………15

Chapter 2 Excavate Trauma……………………18

Chapter 3 Destroy the Myth……………………22

Chapter 4 Amplify the Margin…………………26

Chapter 5 Go Free, Wildflower…………………31

Closing Reflections………………………………34

Word Search…………………………………………39

Crossword Puzzle…………………………………40

Wildflowers

Some of us lost our mothers twice.
We heal through Nommo.
We heal by rewriting our mother's stories.
We liberate our mothers by rewriting their stories.
We create space for them. Untold stories, in worlds (re)imagined.
We reclaim the narratives of our families. We reclaim the narratives of our communities.
With lives lived fully. Untampered. Unabashedly free. Rooted to the earth.

Wildflowers.

We take back the years. Stolen. We heal.
In the spirit of Sankofa, we remember remnants of their souls and we (re)alive them.
Their voices. Their desires. Their pleasures. Their humanness.
Their ambitions before they were tampered with.
Their joy before they were violated. Their innocence before they were robbed.
Before they were taken from us.

Wildflowers.

We hear them as vibrations from their wombs where we lay nuzzled.
Heartbeat to heartbeat. The blood of our blood. We create new imagery.
Untainted. (Un)-Oppressed.
The act of replacing images of our mothers as 'crack mothers' is a liberatory act.
We write to heal. We write to see them as the multidimensional beings they are.
Seeing them and their possible futures.

Wildflowers.

We write for our Grandmothers to reverse and disrupt the pain they felt when they lost their daughters. We write for our Othermothers on bent knees, pressed towards the earth, while praying for their sisters. We reclaim our power in creating space for our mothers.
Our sheroes. Our Ancestors. We create worlds where our mothers can live freely.
Beautifully. Unharmed. Untamed.
Wild and free.
Under a new sun and a willow tree.

Wildflowers.

How to Use This Journal

Dear Black Woman. Black Mother. Black Sister. Black Daughter. *Shapeshifter*. Welcome to the *meeting place*—a safe space for you to wonder, reflect, and create. A space where you can push beyond the boundaries of your imagination by remembering, recovering, and moving forward toward your healing and liberation. The methods and framework outlined in this journal serve as a portal, designed to guide you on a journey toward reclaiming ancestral narratives. Through the Sankofa Writing Method, it is my hope that readers are guided on a path of deep healing and connection to their roots through storytelling. Using the five-step Sankofa Writing Method—**Remember to Talk Back, Excavate Trauma, Destroy the Myth, Amplify the Margin, and Go Free, Wildflower**—you will engage in a process of deep introspection and narrative reconstruction. Each section of this journal provides meditations, practical exercises, and reflective prompts that align with the Sankofa Writing Method. By using these tools, you will find your voice, confront your deepest fears, and shame, and celebrate the beauty of marginal spaces. Through storytelling, you will illustrate how we might change the narrative and create alternative futures for our ancestors as a method of resistance.

This journal offers a blueprint for conceptualizing Black futurity by reconciling traumatic historical realities while reclaiming the voices of our mothers, sisters, and daughters. In this space, we honor the resilience and wisdom of our foremothers, highlighting the importance of remembering and honoring their legacy. It is my fervent wish that readers walk away feeling seen, witnessed, empowered, validated, and with a deeper connection to their ancestors. Your story matters, and you have the power to create positive change in the world. This journal is not just about writing; it is about reclaiming agency and transgressing beyond cultural trauma to prioritize your mental health and healing. As you work through these pages, remember that you are engaging in quilt-work, a powerful tradition of survival and resistance, writing yourself and your loved ones free.

Healing resides in the stories we tell.
Embrace your story.
Honor your ancestors.
Walk boldly in the power of your truth.
You are enough.
You are worthy and deserving of healing and love!
With deepest gratitude and solidarity,
~ Dr. Yannie

Ayana T. Hardaway, Ph.D.
P.S. – Love wrote this book.

Wildflower (noun)~
A term used to describe the speculative reimagining of our ancestors as independent and free. During the process of rewriting ancestral narratives, Wildflowers symbolize our mothers, daughters, and sisters as 'free spirits' who grow and thrive naturally, without being confined by societal expectations or oppression. This reimagining helps counter stereotypes, celebrates their uniqueness, and preserves their truths.

Introduction

There is no time for despair, no place for self-pity, no need for silence, no room for fear. We speak, we write, we do language. That is how civilizations heal. **~ Toni Morrison**

Key Characteristics of the Sankofa Writing Method

The Sankofa Writing Method is a form of freedom technology, a set of tools used to resist oppressive conditions that enable us to survive our present realities. It is a transgressive and transformative tool for coping with and navigating cultural trauma through storytelling while reclaiming ancestral narratives. This method allows us to write through our pain and explore our own judgments and biases. Through this method, we deconstruct our narratives and examine our histories, all while healing and imagining new possibilities and counter-futures for our loved ones. Through this method, we rewrite pieces of our mothers', daughters', and sisters' narratives, reimagining them as Wildflowers—free spirits. By definition, Wildflowers are unbothered, and they grow naturally and freely in the wild, blooming in natural landscapes without any human intervention or cultivation. Metaphorically, the term "Wildflower" describes someone who is independent and unbounded by societal norms and expectations.

In the realm of personal development, healing, and writing futurity for our loved ones, rewriting their lives as Wildflowers is a deliberate disruption and counter to the violence they endured. Reimagining and rewriting their freedom is a deliberate rejection of the stereotypes constructed about them through societal ideologies associated with race, gender, and class oppression. Rewriting our ancestors as Wildflowers allows us to reimagine their uniqueness, truths, and ability to thrive without adversity.

Key characteristics of this writing method includes leaving everything on the page, deconstructing dominant narratives, connecting emotions to events, and reclaiming agency and power through storytelling. This immersive process helps us piece ourselves back together, retaining authorship over our lives. The meaning of the word "Transgress" means to "Step across or beyond." This is why we are here. We are here to write ourselves free by *crossing over, to, through, and beyond* our trauma, our deepest fears, and our shame. Writing to transgress means that you are ready to prioritize your mental health and acknowledge your trauma so that you can start your healing journey.

The term Sankofa is a West African word with origins from the Akan tribe in Ghana, which translates to "To go back and fetch it," symbolizing the importance of remembering and obtaining knowledge from your past in order to move forward. The interpretation used within this method amplifies the significance of our quest for knowledge, remembering that our pasts must never be forgotten. To move toward a progressive future, we must know where we come from. This practice and this tradition have been indicative of our survival.

The Sankofa Writing Method Framework

The Sankofa Writing Method is a five-step framework that situates writing as a practice of freedom and healing spaces where we can push beyond the boundaries of our imaginations by remembering, recovering, and moving forward toward our liberation. The five-step framework includes the following:

1. Remember to Talk Back
2. Excavate Trauma
3. Destroy the Myth
4. Amplify the Margin
5. Go Free, Wildflower

Remembering to Talk Back is about finding your voice, confronting your shadows, and deconstructing your beliefs. This step requires us to actively seek out knowledge so that we can speak up assertively to challenge norms, and systemic oppression.

Excavating Trauma requires us to dig deep and take inventory of our memories so that we can unravel the roots of our histories and engage our deepest fears and our shame head-on. Through this process of excavation, we peel back the layers of intergenerational trauma, societal injustices, and historical legacies that have shaped our experiences. By identifying critical traumatic events, we lay the groundwork for healing and eventual reconstruction of ourselves and our stories.

Destroying the Myth is about our insistence to lift the veil and stay as close to our ancestors' truth as possible by centering them as victims and challenging dominant worldviews and perspectives about them. Through self-definition, recovering ancestral truth refers to the process of rediscovering and reclaiming authentic narratives and experiences that may have been obscured or suppressed by external influences, societal norms, or personal trauma. This step requires you to set aside your feelings and seek knowledge so that you can challenge your beliefs.

Amplifying the Margin deals with finding the silver lining—and recognizing the beauty that resides in marginal spaces through the rich cultural tradition of Black families and Black women-centered networks nurturing and caring for one another as a sacred and cultural practice. Amplifying the margin is about cherishing and capturing moments when our ancestors experienced being cared for, joy, pleasure, and love as empowering and validating experiences.

Go free, Wildflower captures the final culminating step where we liberate our ancestors. In this step, we integrate all that we have learned through our journey to creatively write our liberation, drawing from Black speculative and Afrofuturist conventions. In this step, we *write our ancestors free*.

The Sankofa Writing Method Toolkit

While perceiving futurity, it is important to allow your radical imagination to run free, so I have designed the Sankofa Writing Method toolkit to inspire and spark creative ideation for your writing as a sacred practice. Below are a few examples of ways to incorporate Black speculative and Afrofuturist conventions through your writing and storytelling:

- Literary Restoration: Through our writing as a sacred practice, we safeguard the legacy of our ancestors and transcend the white gaze by focusing on reclaiming their narratives. This sacred endeavor prohibits the perpetuation of harm and the infliction of violence or stress upon our ancestors' bodies through our storytelling, whether written or spoken. Engaging in this intentional practice is a tribute to honor and show reverence to our ancestors.

- Empowering Marginalized Voices: Afrofuturism amplifies marginalized voices, providing a platform to share our own stories on our own terms. By centering the experiences and perspectives of Black characters, Afrofuturist writing challenges dominant narratives and celebrates diversity.

- Bending Time: This method of writing does not conform to Western and Eurocentric perceptions of time. Chronology is an illusion. Through *Sankofa*, we bend time and untie the years. We go backward, forward, upward, and downward. We wrap our arms around future generations. We occupy four-dimensional space. Time is malleable, circular, cyclical, and synchronous—which stimulates creative and imaginative futures. Time is agreed upon through our communion—and our collective agreement.

- Speculative Futures: Through an Afrofuturist lens, we can envision future societies where Black people play central and empowered roles as agents. This can involve imagining advanced civilizations built upon Afrocentric principles, exploring themes of innovation and liberation.

The Sankofa Writing Method Toolkit

- Centering African Mythology and Folklore: Afrofuturist writing often draws inspiration from African mythology and folklore—weaving together ancient stories, tales, songs, and legends into futuristic narratives. By incorporating elements of traditional African spirituality and cosmology, we can reimagine nuanced worlds for our ancestors that center and honor Black cultural traditions.

- Critiquing Power Structures: Using a speculative lens provides a platform for critiquing contemporary power structures and systemic injustices. As writers, we can use speculative fiction to explore themes of oppression, resistance, and social change, offering alternative visions of justice and liberation.

- Exploring Technology and Innovation: Afrofuturism embraces technology as a tool for empowerment and liberation. Writers can explore scientific technologies, and innovative digital cultures within their narratives, imagining how these developments intersect with African and Black diasporic experiences.

- Be Creative: Have fun and utilize this method in any way that inspire you. These are broad concepts on ways that you can creatively apply the method through writing as an art form. The boundaries are limitless, so use this time to really stretch your imagination and let your radical mind run free.

Applying The Sankofa Writing Method

Affirmation
I release feelings of shame around my identity

Putting Concepts into Action

☐ Throughout this writing process, it is important to prioritize your mental health needs, and this looks different for everyone. Below are examples of practices you can adopt in your healing journey:

☐ Self-Care: Dedicate "you-time" to activities that promote relaxation and reduce stress, such as exercise, meditation, scheduling a massage *because you deserve it*, yoga, or other hobbies.

☐ Seek Support: Reach out to friends, family members, or mental health professionals for emotional support and guidance when needed. For some, connecting with a licensed professional with shared cultural experiences is essential for establishing a meaningful connection to explore cultural trauma. This was a requirement for me. This process can be cathartic for some individuals while triggering for others. Seeking support from a professional clinician is always a wise decision.

☐ Practice Mindfulness: Engage in mindfulness techniques to stay present and manage overwhelming thoughts or emotions effectively.

☐ Setting Boundaries: Set boundaries within your networks to help safeguard your personal space, time, and resources. Protecting your peace during this journey allows you to stay focused on your healing while prioritizing self-care, hobbies, and responsibilities without feeling obligated to constantly meet others' demands.

Writing Prompts

- ☐ Reflect on your sources of trauma and consider how resolving them could positively impact your life. Use your audio recorder app or journaling as a tool to document your responses.
  _____
  _____
  _____

- ☐ How do you currently prioritize self-care in your daily life? Are there any additional self-care practices you would like to incorporate?
  _____
  _____
  _____
  _____

- ☐ Reflect on your sources of trauma from childhood or observations of trauma, whether indirect or direct. Describe these experiences in detail, including how they have affected you.
  _____
  _____
  _____

- ☐ Explore the emotional and psychological effects of your trauma. Write about any patterns or behaviors that have emerged as a result and how they have influenced your life.
  _____
  _____
  _____

- ☐ Imagine a future where you have healed from your trauma. Describe what this future looks like and how it differs from your current circumstances.
  _____
  _____
  _____
  _____

Chapter 1: Remember to Talk Back

Moving from silence into speech is for the oppressed, the colonized, the exploited, and...it is that act of speech, of "talking back" that is no mere gesture of empty words, that is the expression of moving from object to subject, that is the liberated voice.
~ bell hooks

Applying The Sankofa Writing Method

Affirmation
My story is powerful, and I am ready to speak my truth

Putting Concepts into Action

This chapter discussed the importance of finding your voice, confronting shadows, and examining personal beliefs as crucial aspects of the healing journey. Drawing on bell hooks' concept of *"talking back"* as a form of resistance, it emphasizes the significance of articulating your story and challenging societal norms that silence marginalized groups, namely Black women. The chapter explores the process of confronting internalized beliefs and shadows, particularly regarding the portrayal of Black crack mothers and the crack baby myth. Now, it is your turn to apply what you have learned.

Writing Prompts

- ☐ Reflect on your shadows by identifying traits or aspects of yourself that you suppress or reject. How do these shadows manifest in your life, and what steps can you take to integrate them?

_____
_____
_____
_____
_____
_____
_____

Writing Prompts

☐ Consider the concept of *"talking back"* as a form of resistance. How can expressing your truth challenge dominant power structures and reclaim agency?

_____
_____
_____
_____

☐ Consider a narrative or stereotype that has been perpetuated by societal norms or historical accounts. How has this narrative shaped your understanding of your family history?

_____
_____
_____
_____

☐ What gaps in knowledge are needed to help challenge your beliefs about your ancestors?

_____
_____
_____
_____

☐ Investigate the impact of societal stereotypes and controlling images on your identity and sense of self-worth. How have these representations influenced your perceptions of yourself and your ancestors?

_____
_____
_____
_____

☐ Analyze the crack baby myth and its portrayal in the media. How has misinformation affected your personal beliefs?

Chapter 2: Excavate Trauma

Black women have had to develop a larger vision of our society than perhaps any other group. They have had to understand white men, white women, and Black men. And they have had to understand themselves. When Black women win victories, it is a boost for virtually every segment of society.
~ Angela Davis

Applying The Sankofa Writing Method

Affirmation
I release myself from past mistakes and embrace forgiveness as a path to healing and growth

Putting Concepts into Action

This chapter serves as a guide for excavating and navigating critical traumatic incidents, inviting readers to embark on a transformative journey of self-discovery and healing through the power of memory work. Now, it is your turn to apply the method by detailing critical traumatic incidents from your life. Remember, I focus on the crack epidemic to track my application of the method stemming from trauma tied to my mother's addiction. Apply this step toward any form of cultural trauma that you would like to work on and heal from. Begin by taking inventory of memories that were traumatic for you. You might also choose a memory that does not include a parent or loved one because they were not there. Maybe they could not be there because they transitioned too soon, or were slain at the hand of gun violence, or they overdosed at the height of their suffering, or were incarcerated. You might decide to choose a milestone. For example, my mother was not present for any milestone that I have ever had in my entire life. I am talking about elementary school assemblies, choir performances, award ceremonies, graduations, sporting events, my wedding, and the birth of my children. My mother was not able to share any of these moments with me. If you have similar moments in your life, and the absence of your ancestor was traumatic for you, and you would like to explore that, then use it. Whatever it is. Name it for yourself and use this method as a tool that works for you.

Mindfulness Exercise

Find a comfortable seated position either in a chair with your feet flat on the ground or if you prefer, you can sit with your legs crossed on the floor or using a cushion. Close your eyes.

Begin by bringing your awareness to a critical traumatic incident that you have experienced. Allow the memory to come into your mind without judgment or resistance. Notice how this memory feels in your body. Pay attention to any sensations of tension, tightness, or discomfort that arise as you recall the incident.

Take slow, deep breaths, inhaling through your nose and exhaling through your mouth.

What color is the memory?
What energy does this memory have?
What emotion does this memory invoke?
What does the room feel like?
How do you feel at this moment?
If there are others in this memory, how are they feeling in this moment?
What do you think they are thinking about?
How do you feel about your ancestors in this memory?
How does everyone around you feel about your ancestor in this moment?
Think about the way you felt.
Tap into the energy of yourself in that memory.
Start from where you are.

With each exhale, imagine yourself releasing any stress or tension. As you continue to breathe deeply, focus on the areas of your body where you feel stress or discomfort. Send your breath to these areas, allowing them to soften and relax with each breath.

Notice any thoughts or emotions that arise as you engage in this practice. Acknowledge them without judgment, and then gently guide your focus back to your breath. Consider the sensory details of this moment and visualize the physical environment.

Repeat this process of deep breathing and body awareness for several minutes, allowing yourself to fully experience the present moment without becoming overwhelmed by the memory.

When you feel ready, slowly open your eyes, and return your awareness to your surroundings.

Take a moment to notice how you feel after completing this meditation.

Writing Prompts

☐ List a *critical traumatic incident* that surfaced during your meditation about your ancestor. If several memories surfaced, just focus on writing about one for this activity.

_____
_____
_____
_____

☐ Consider the sensory details of this moment: What happened? What did it feel like? What did it smell like? Take note of any colors, textures, or sensations.

_____
_____
_____
_____

☐ Visualize the physical environment: Think about the details of the space you were in. Was the floor hard or soft? What color was the carpet? Who else was there? How did you and others in the room feel? What was said or exchanged during this moment?

_____
_____
_____
_____

☐ Write as much as you can. Try to write up to one page.
Engage deeply with the memory: Allow yourself to fully immerse in the experience and be present in the moment.

Once done, you can repeat the process for other *critical traumatic incidents*, focusing on uncovering the nuances and details of each experience. Reflect on the insights gained from revisiting these memories and consider compiling a list of key takeaways or realizations.

☐ Excellent job! This healing journey is not easy, and we just covered a difficult step. Do not be ashamed to cry thug tears if you need to. Baby, I spent most of 2023 crying tears of pain, sorrow, and joy. You are brave, and you are worthy. Remember, you are not alone.
Keep going. It only gets better.

Chapter 3: Destroy the Myths

Where does a Black woman go when she is me, trailed by myths that this country has invented about her? Where to go to, when all of you have been there already, and claimed the turf as your own and you watch the rest of us shipwrecked by circumstance and color, looking. Waiting. Needing.
~ Sonia Sanchez

Applying The Sankofa Writing Method

Affirmation
I affirm my commitment to preserving and celebrating the truth of my ancestors' experiences

Putting Concepts into Action

In this chapter, we explored the powerful act of dispelling myths surrounding ourselves and our ancestors as a form of resistance and reclaiming their true identities. I shared my journey of identifying the myths I had internalized and those propagated by society about myself and my mother. Recognizing that these beliefs were based on falsehoods, I delved into the truth, viewing her addiction scientifically as a medical condition and chronic illness. By piecing together memories and stories from those close to her, I began to see a more holistic picture of who she truly was. In this chapter, we covered the importance of honoring our ancestors' humanity and preserving their legacies. Through this process, we rise above the constraints of addiction, allowing the genuine essence of our loved ones to shine. Your task is to explore the authentic truth of your ancestors, uncovering insights and understanding from a fresh perspective. Each detail revealed brings us closer to reclaiming and honoring their true essence. Now, it is your turn to apply these lessons and embark on your own journey of discovery.

Chapter 3: Destroy the Myths

Mapping Your Myths

It is important that we name our beliefs so that we may examine them. Using the following chart, begin to make a list of the myths that you subscribe to for yourself and your ancestor within the center of the circle. In the outer circle labeled 'margin,' begin to write what was actually true based on what you learned and what you remembered about your ancestor.

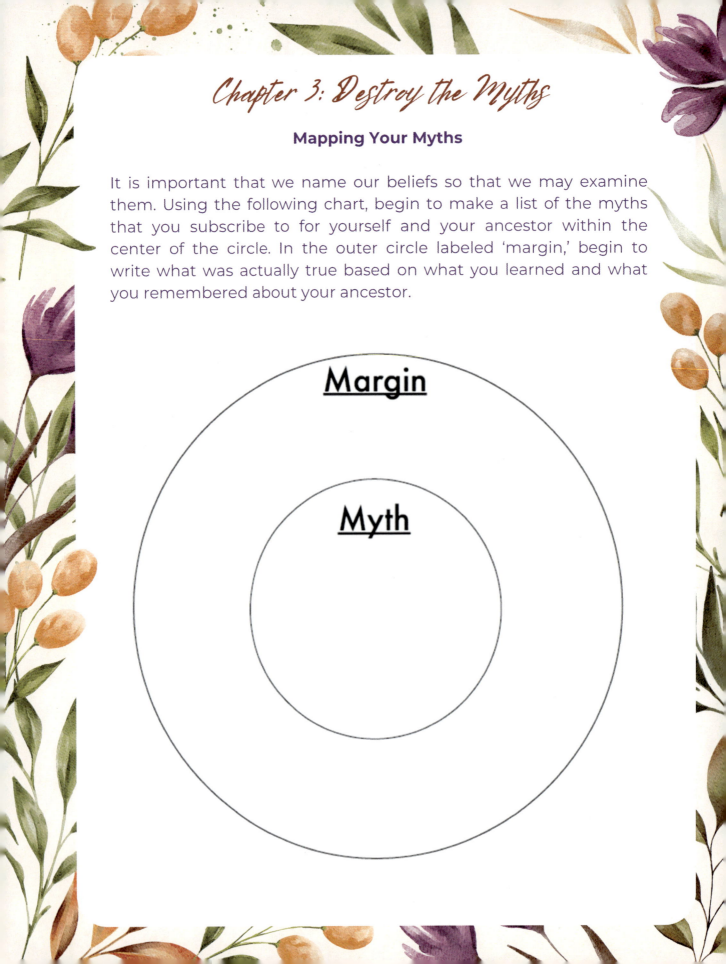

Writing Prompts

- ☐ Write a list of at least three individuals who could help fill the void and provide you with truth about your ancestors before their struggle with addiction. Consider speaking with family members, friends, or coworkers of your loved one who may hold valuable insights into your ancestor's life. If you want to speak with more than three people, go for it. The goal is to get as close to the truth as possible.

  _____
  _____
  _____
  _____

- ☐ Next, you should craft a series of questions aimed at uncovering various aspects of your ancestor's identity and experiences before their addiction. Delve deep into their childhood, favorite songs, cherished memories, and personality traits. Spend some time thinking about exactly what it is you want to know. For example, in the seventies, my mother impulsively moved to Los Angeles, California with her boyfriend who was a musician and lived there for a short while. Wild and free. I also moved to California pretty abruptly with my family because we wanted a new life. This was always ironic and interesting to me, so I asked others about my mother's move to California. Be intentional in your questions. You will be amazed by the information you will uncover.

  _____
  _____
  _____
  _____

- ☐ Schedule dedicated time to meet with the individuals on your list. Approach these conversations with an open heart and a genuine curiosity for learning about your ancestor's life. Take note of the insights shared and the stories recounted, recognizing each detail uncovered as a valuable step towards reclaiming and honoring your ancestor's truth. If you feel comfortable, ask if you can record the conversation.

☐ Reflect on the process of exploring your ancestor's life, pre-addiction. Consider how these insights have deepened your understanding of their identity and enriched your connection to your family's history. How do these newfound revelations shape your perception of your ancestor and their journey? How do these newfound revelations shape you and your journey?

Chapter 4: Amplify The Margin

The single story creates stereotypes, and the problem with stereotypes is not that they are untrue, but that they are incomplete. They make one story become the only story.
~ Chimamanda Ngozi Adichie

Applying The Sankofa Writing Method

Affirmation
I honor and cherish the legacy of my ancestors, recognizing their resilience and their sacrifices.

Putting Concepts into Action

In this section, we capture our ancestors from a holistic view by amplifying marginal experiences which center the voices of the oppressed. Through the process of amplifying our ancestors' truth, I explore the imperative of correcting and making right the narratives that have been silenced or misrepresented while honoring their humanity. By amplifying the marginal experiences from my childhood, I elevate my mother's story, which is that she was cared for, catered to, cherished, nurtured, pampered, and protected by our family. Beauty resides in the margins. The business of redressing our ancestors requires us to acknowledge their victimhood and honor their humanity amidst the adversity they faced. I have shared my truth. Now it is your turn.

Chapter 4: Amplify The Margin

Gratitude Meditation Exercises

Find a comfortable and quiet place to sit or lie down. Close your eyes and take a few deep breaths to center yourself. Think of someone or something for which you are deeply grateful.
It could be an ancestor, a loved one, a friend, or a cherished memory.
As you focus on this person or thing, allow yourself to fully experience the feelings of gratitude and appreciation. Notice any sensations in your body, such as warmth, openness, or lightness.
Now, silently repeat a series of phrases expressing gratitude towards this person or thing.
You can use phrases like:
"Thank you for being a part of my life."
"I am grateful for the love and support you provide."
"Your presence brings me joy and happiness."
Continue to repeat these phrases, allowing them to resonate deeply within you.
Stay in this state of gratitude for as long as you feel comfortable
When you are ready to conclude the meditation, take a few more deep breaths and slowly bring your awareness back to the present moment.

Open your eyes and carry the sense of gratitude with you as you go about your day.

Chapter 4: Amplify The Margin

Mapping the Margins of Our Ancestors' Truths

It is time to shift marginal experiences so that we may position them back to their proper subject place. It is time to shift them to the center. In the chart below, rewrite the list of your beliefs about your ancestors to honor their truth. You can use words or phrases like *"cared for," "loved by many,"* and you can describe them as *"beautiful."* In my chart, I wrote down that my mother is a grandmother. Although she transitioned many years ago, it does not make this truth any less of a truth. My children know of their grandmother Tremayne, so it is important for me to capture this identifier as her truth. I also used words like *creative, animal lover, beautiful, impulsive, musician, deep thinker, big sister, little sister, Aunt, giver, kind, expressive, playful, trusting, and innocent.*

Truth

Writing Prompts

- ☐ Identify and reflect on marginal experiences and moments when your ancestor experienced being cared for, joy, pleasure, and love as empowering and validating experiences.

_____
_____
_____
_____

- ☐ What new insights or perspectives have you gained about amplifying marginalized experiences through this chapter?
How can we continue to challenge and disrupt harmful narratives about addiction in popular culture?

_____
_____
_____
_____

- ☐ Consider the idea of reframing marginal positions in your own life. Are there narratives or beliefs about yourself or your family history that you would like to correct or challenge?

_____
_____
_____
_____

- ☐ In what ways can storytelling and narratives be used as tools for social justice and inclusivity in conversations about addiction and recovery?

_____
_____
_____
_____

☐ What emotions arise for you when considering the humanity of individuals who struggle with addiction, particularly in the context of personal relationships?

Chapter 5: Go Free, Wildflower

Paradise is one's own place, One's own people, One's own world, Knowing and known, Perhaps even loving, and loved.
~ Octavia E. Butler

Applying The Sankofa Writing Method

Affirmation
The legacy of my ancestors lives on through me as I embrace their teachings and carry their love forward.

Putting Concepts into Action

Now, it is your turn to apply what you have learned. Use what you have learned about the writing characteristics of the Sankofa Writing Method. Refer to the Sankofa Writing Method in the Introduction. Through your creative storytelling, you can blend elements of science fiction, fantasy, mythology, African futurity, and your ancestor's truth to envision bold and imaginative futures:

Grounding Meditation Exercise

Hold your mother in your mind for a few minutes
Think of her
Imagine her free
What languages does she speak?
What does her hair look like?
Is she alone, or is she with another ancestor?
What is she doing?
What is she wearing?
How old is she?
What are her superpowers?
What is her favorite color?
Does she prefer Kale or Collards?
Where does she like to go?
What are her secrets?
What gives her pleasure?
Who does she spend her time with?
What planet would she visit?
Where does she live?
What does she like to eat/drink?
What is her personality like?
What would she tell you?

Writing Prompts

- [ ] With these reflections in mind, begin to write freely. Allow your thoughts and emotions to flow onto the page, guided by the imagery you just created through this grounding exercise.

_____
_____
_____
_____

- [ ] You can choose to reimagine a counter-history or future by using one of the critical traumatic incidents you identified in Chapter three: Excavating Truth. The objective here is to replace the traumatic event with an alternative version that centers on your ancestor's liberation and resilience.

_____
_____
_____
_____

- [ ] You may choose to reimagine a counter-history or future from scratch that is not tied to any specific event in your life. You may choose to write what feels organic for you.

_____
_____
_____
_____

- [ ] As you rewrite each narrative, infuse it with all the nuggets of truths you collected along your journey. Incorporate everything! This is your opportunity to make Wildflower gumbo!

  This process has been heavy, but now that we are on the other side of it, it is time to create. Using all that has been collected, begin to write your ancestor free!

  Last but certainly not least. Go off!

Closing Reflections

It is imperative that we, as Black women, talk about the experiences that shaped us; that we assess our strengths and weaknesses and define our own history. It is imperative that we discuss positive ways to teach and socialize our children... Let us rebuild the culture of giving and carry on the tradition of fierce determination to move on closer to freedom.
~ Assata Shakur

Moving Forward

We made it. You made it. You have journeyed through the depths of freedom, dreaming, healing, and growth. You Shapeshifted so that you could heal yourself. You have reached the other side, and I could not be prouder of you. You have done the difficult and daunting work of acknowledging your shadow and confronting your cultural trauma. Not only that—you have rewritten it. You have reshaped the narrative, reclaiming agency for yourself and your ancestors. Through your courage and resilience, you have reframed the context in which your trauma existed. You destroyed the myths and amplified the margins. You did this, and you did not need anyone's permission to do so except for your own. This is an incredible achievement, and I applaud your bravery, and your vulnerability.

The Sankofa Writing Method has been transformative in my life and has completely shifted my perspective. It has changed how I think about my mother, other Black women, and other Black and Brown people who truly were victims of this American tragedy and other forms of cultural trauma. This process has changed how I talk about my mother; it has changed how I talk about my mother to my children. As a scholar, it has shifted my perspectives on how we examine divergent or marginal experiences and narratives within historical contexts. I believe there's healing in truth. For me, my personal healing journey enabled me to combine my love for scholarship, art, creative writing, and theorizing to develop a culturally informed speculative framework that will help others to heal.

Closing Reflections

Thank you for joining me on this journey. Gratitude for trusting me and allowing me to share pieces of my truth to track how I came to this work.

Now that you have completed this process, it is time to decide what comes next. For some, internal healing may be sufficient, and there's no obligation to share your story with others. You may decide that your work here is done. For those who feel called to share, consider this an opportunity to initiate conversations with loved ones or family members. Use your experience and the tools provided in this book as a starting point for dialogue. Your story can serve as a portal to healing for others, offering them insight, and understanding into their own experiences.

As you embark on this next phase of your journey, remember that your ability to impact others is linked to your willingness to dig deep. By sharing your truth, you have the power to heal and inspire those around you. Some may even feel compelled to follow in your footsteps and share their own stories of healing and resilience. To those who are ready to take the bold step of sharing their stories, I invite you to join me in healing others. Let us be disruptors, reclaiming our ancestral tongues and empowering others through the power of storytelling. Together, we can create a ripple effect of healing and transformation that extends far beyond ourselves.
With deepest gratitude and solidarity,

~ Dr. Yannie
Ayana T. Hardaway, Ph.D.
P.S. – Love wrote this book.

Closing Reflections
Applying The Sankofa Writing Method

Affirmation
I cultivate inner peace and resilience, embracing my heritage as a source of strength and healing

Putting Concepts into Action

As we go forward, we continue the tradition. This is the essence of quilt work, as we recreate new narratives under new suns. We stand as proverbial botanists, sowing seeds of wisdom and strength into the hearts of our children. This profound healing journey calls us to remember the ancient guidance of our foremothers, who have laid the groundwork for our resilience in times of adversity. Let us continue their legacy through the radical act of storytelling, healing, and community building. Together, let us continue to cultivate a community of healing, strength, and empowerment. Your story is a vital thread in the fabric of our collective resilience.

Reflections & Next Steps

- Reflect on your healing journey and the insights gained through the Sankofa Writing Method. Write about how you have integrated these insights into your life and relationships.

- How do you envision your future now that you have taken intentional steps towards your journey in healing and reclaiming your ancestral narratives?

- How has using Black speculative fiction and Afrofuturist elements empowered you to reimagine the lives of your ancestors and envision futures free from oppression?

- Reflect on the profound experience of being witnessed and validated in your healing journey. How does sharing your stories contribute to your sense of connection and resilience?

- Take a courageous step forward by sharing your stories with trusted friends, family members, or a clinical professional.

- Create healing spaces within your own family and social networks to start dialogue free from judgment about your loved ones.

Crossword Puzzle

ACROSS
3. Terms used to refer to young Black girls, emphasizing their innocence and rejecting adult stereotypes placed on them.
6. A way of thinking created by Molefi Kete Asante that focuses on Black people's experiences within their own cultural and historical contexts.
7. A West African term meaning "to go back and fetch it," highlighting the importance of learning from the past to move forward.
8. Work: Using writing and storytelling to honor the tradition of quilting in the Black community, symbolizing survival, and resistance.
9. A concept by bell hooks describing places of resistance and strength for marginalized people
10. Alternative visions of the future that challenge mainstream ideas and aim to create better outcomes.
11. A resistance method using spiritual and Indigenous knowledge to adapt and survive, involving control over one's body and actions.
12. Trauma effects that are passed down through generations.
13. A theory combining Black feminism and Afrofuturism to explore how speculative fiction can help Black women and girls achieve success and liberation.
14. Reflecting on and understanding one's past experiences and suppressed traumas.
15. Tools used to resist oppression and survive current realities.

DOWN
1. A period in the 1980s and 1990s marked by widespread crack cocaine addiction and its devastating impact on Black communities.
2. Memories or experiences that cause trauma from direct or indirect exposure to traumatic events.
4. The collective distress a community feels after a significant, painful event that affects their identity and beliefs.
5. A term used to describe the speculative reimagining of our ancestors as independent and free.

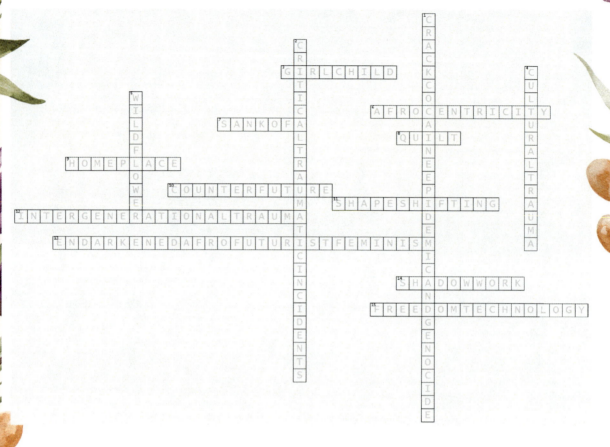

ACROSS
3. Terms used to refer to young Black girls, emphasizing their innocence and rejecting adult stereotypes placed on them.
6. A way of thinking created by Molefi Kete Asante that focuses on Black people's experiences within their own cultural and historical contexts.
7. A West African term meaning "to go back and fetch it," highlighting the importance of learning from the past to move forward.
8. Work: Using writing and storytelling to honor the tradition of quilting in the Black community, symbolizing survival, and resistance.
9. A concept by bell hooks describing places of resistance and strength for marginalized people.
10. Alternative visions of the future that challenge mainstream ideas and aim to create better outcomes.
11. A resistance method using spiritual and Indigenous knowledge to adapt and survive, involving control over one's body and actions.
12. Trauma effects that are passed down through generations.
13. A theory combining Black feminism and Afrofuturism to explore how speculative fiction can help Black women and girls achieve success and liberation.
14. Reflecting on and understanding one's past experiences and suppressed traumas.
15. Tools used to resist oppression and survive current realities.

DOWN
1. A period in the 1980s and 1990s marked by widespread crack cocaine addiction and its devastating impact on Black communities.
2. Memories or experiences that cause trauma from direct or indirect exposure to traumatic events.
4. The collective distress a community feels after a significant, painful event that affects their identity and beliefs.
5. A term used to describe the speculative reimagining of our ancestors as independent and free.

Word Search Puzzle

```
B B T D Z X A R X A F H F G E N O C I D E J K A Q O D T R
S C O N W H B R Z I X U U M I X T P U P U H H C B R M M J
E J C I M E D I P E E N I A C O C K C A R C N O E B W H T
D C Y T I C I R T N E C O R F A O J W C D W D W J H J W R
W K W H V Y C O U N T E R F U T U R E S B O O F T F R K I
W L B J M K T C C B P A L N Z G Y Y A L E L D C W U R M B
W F E G Z F A H H U J I S D B E W N G I F X R X Z V T W C
T T M D C P J O H Q T I I X O O K M B D G T C K P O S P P
F E L H A C M F U Y O I U Z J O J I L N Z G H H D C L R S
M R X R P E V I T L J V C C F V D I V Q N R N I Q K P X Q
R F J B P K L M E H Q Y Y A X Z W H L I G Z Q I T Q Y W D
K K O L J T M J C S D R D K E O M F T Q M B X N D J G U A
Q N A J W W S E B F P V N E M B T F N P P Q A H B I M G H
T C U O Z I I K H Z C H X C A A I K K R O W W O D A H S J
E M R L H C U L R T D W F G O H K K H N Y V L Z X Y H W G
U K B F S U U R F Y D G D A S Q J A W A Y E J G P R Q I U
N B G L P H E Y Z F M Y K E P D S B K T H B Q I A U J W C
J P O B M L B N V P G B P V T U R A O J G C Z M S X B E N
L J T N V I P P Y W H A J T J T Z Q G L R Z C J P T T I G
O L B J Y G O L O N H C E T M O D E E R F I A W O I I G Y
R F W X R G T X Z S B F Z R I S L J T D W Z B R Z F L X M
E C R I T I C A L T R A U M A T I C I N C I D E N T S C J
M S P G I R L C H I L D G I R L C H I L D R E N Q C U O L
W M M I F B K F L S K L Q Y E R T N I Y W E L Y E U H T Q
D G K Y F J Z U N Z T I T I A M U A R T L A R U T L U C F
S F O J E A T U K P P R V J I C A A I G U V Z I F C T R Z
F G Q I N T E R G E N E R A T I O N A L T R A U M A M T S
O O J E C D S R O N Z I S N U Y M C V H B J J H C P M T J
X Y O X V X M P U Q Y Z Q W Q E E D C A H M O J S R B G S
```

AFROCENTRICITY
CRACK COCAINE EPIDEMIC
CRITICAL TRAUMATIC INCIDENTS
CULTURAL TRAUMA
GENOCIDE
HOMEPLACE
QUILT WORK
SHADOW WORK
WILDFLOWER

COUNTER FUTURE

FREEDOM TECHNOLOGY
GIRLCHILD/GIRLCHILDREN
INTERGENERATIONAL TRAUMA
SANKOFA
SHAPESHIFTING

Word Search Puzzle Solution

Made in the USA
Middletown, DE
10 October 2024

62332165R00029